STEP-UP
GEOGRAPHY

What's in the news?

Ruth Nason & Julia Roche

Evans

Published by Evans Brothers Limited
2A Portman Mansions
Chiltern Street
London W1U 6NR

© Evans Brothers Limited 2005

Produced for Evans Brothers Limited by
White-Thomson Publishing Ltd,
Bridgewater Business Centre,
210 High Street,
Lewes, East Sussex BN7 2NH

Printed in China by New Era Printing Co. Ltd

Project manager: Ruth Nason

Designer: Helen Nelson, Jet the Dog

Consultant: John Lace, School Improvement
Manager, Hampshire County Council

Cover: Main and top left photographs by Chris
Fairclough; top right photo by Bryan Knox/Papilio.

Website addresses included in this book were
valid at the time of going to press. The Publishers
cannot take responsibility for later changes in
location or content.

British Library Cataloguing in Publication Data

Nason, Ruth

What's in the news?. - (Step-up geography)
1.Geography - Press coverage - Juvenile literature
2.Mass media in education - Juvenile literature

I. Title II.Roche, Julia

070.4,4991

ISBN: 0 237 528819

Special thanks to St Dominic's School, Harpenden,
for their help and involvement in the preparation
of this book.

Picture acknowledgements:

Corbis: pages 4tl and 9 (Joe Skipper/Reuters),
4cl and 24 (David Turnley), 4cr and 21 (Bobby
Yip/Reuters), 6t (Pablo Sanchez/Reuters), 6b (Ian
Hodgson/Reuters), 7 (Martin Bennett/Reuters), 8t
(Mike Fincke/NASA), 8b (Claudia Daut/Reuters),
13t (Matthieu Paley), 14 (Gary Braasch), 15t (Roger
Ressmeyer), 17 (Liu Liqun), 23 (Barclay Graham/
Corbis Sygma), 24b (Peter Morgan/Reuters), 25
(Janet Jarman); Chris Fairclough: pages 1, 4bl, 5,
11b, 13b, 16tl, 16tr, 18r, 19, 22l, 22r, 27; Chris
Fairclough Photo Library: pages 4tc, 4tr, 12b, 26b;
Michael Nason: page 18l; Papilio: pages 20t (Bryan
Knox), 20b (Pat Jerrold); Jean Peyton: page 16b.

Maps and diagrams by Helen Nelson.

Contents

Geography in the news

USA

UK

UK

Somalia

China

Newspapers and news reports on radio, television and the internet all give us information about recent events. The news may be local (about the area where you live), national (about your country) or international (about other countries).

When you hear about places on the news and don't know where they are, see if you can find them on a map or in an atlas. Some news reports include a map. Often there are pictures to show what the place is like.

▼ *What local papers are there for your town or village and* county? *Do any have the same names as these?*

▲ *You could make a class display, attaching pictures from the international news to the appropriate parts of a large world map.*

Some news reports are about subjects that you learn about in Geography. For example:

- unusual or extreme weather;

- natural disasters, such as earthquakes and volcanoes;

- changes that people are making to their environment, such as building a new road;

- environmental issues, such as pollution, deforestation and endangered animals.

▶ *These children saw news reports about a* hurricane. *To understand more, they looked in atlases, encyclopedias and other books.*

Your Geography work can help you to understand the news, and the news can help you to think about your Geography work and see that it is part of real life.

Why do people like to find out about the news?

Many people read, watch or listen to the news at least once a day. Ask some people you know if they do this, and why.

Local information – for example, about roadworks that are starting – can be very useful.

Events in other places can help us to think about situations in our own locality.

Often the news seems to be about bad things, but there are hopeful news items too – about new discoveries or people's achievements.

It can be fascinating to learn about places very different from our own country.

What happens in one country can affect places all around the world. So we need to follow the news and try to understand it.

The weather in the news

You could collect news stories about a Geography theme, such as the weather.

Freak weather

Sometimes the weather is in the news because it is different from expected – for example, very warm in winter in the UK. Sometimes it is in the news because it beats a record: for example, the hottest summer day or the deepest snow for 50 years.

▶ *What news headline would you write to go with a photograph of heavy snow?*

▼ *This photograph could illustrate a news story that unusually wet summer weather has damaged many farmers' crops.*

Headline writer

Written news reports always have a headline, which sums up what has happened and attracts attention. Try writing some headlines for some possible news items about the weather.

RAIN STOPS PLAY

MIDSUMMER MELTDOWN

Weather effects

Some news stories are about the effect of the weather. For example, rain can:

- stop a sports match;
- reduce sales of summer clothes;
- spoil a farmer's crops.

Weather disasters

Floods, drought and hurricanes can cause misery to large numbers of people. In August 2004 the village of Boscastle in Cornwall was flooded. Boscastle became the main news in national newspapers and news programmes. The report shown here is from the day after the flood. See if you can draw a simple map to go with the report. Which places will you show?

Notice how the report gives information about:

- what has happened;
- where;
- how people are affected;
- why it happened;
- what is likely to happen next.

NO DEATHS IN BOSCASTLE FLOOD

The chief constable of Devon and Cornwall has said it was a 'miracle' that no one died yesterday in the flooded village of Boscastle.

More than a hundred people were evacuated and eight were treated for conditions ranging from hypothermia to broken bones after a three-metre-high wall of water swept down a steep valley into the Atlantic.

The village stands where two valleys meet, and so it was badly affected when one month's rain fell in less than two hours.

The water swept fallen trees, branches, stones and rubble down Boscastle's steep streets at 40 mph.

People cannot yet go back to their homes, to see the damage.

Forecasters predict bad weather for the rest of

Britain this week as the knock-on effects of Tropical Storm Bonnie bring strong winds and heavy rain.

Bonnie picked up speed in the Gulf of Mexico last week. As it moved past North Carolina, the storm span off tornadoes which killed three people, injured 20, damaged buildings and caused power cuts.

The hurricane season

From June to November people in some parts of the world expect tropical storms. Look for news about these in late summer and early autumn.

Storm names

Tropical storms are spinning masses of thunderclouds, blown from near the equator towards the poles. When a storm travels faster than 38 mph, it is given a name, like Tropical Storm Bonnie. At more than 74 mph it is called a hurricane, like Hurricane Ivan.

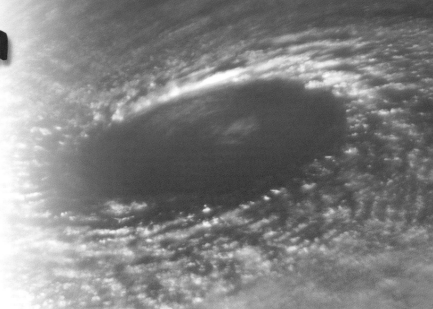

▲ *This photograph of Hurricane Ivan was taken from space.*

The first five tropical storms or hurricanes in the Atlantic in 2004 were named Alex, Bonnie, Charley, Danielle and Earl. What do you notice about the names? Meteorologists use several sets of names like these for tropical storms in different parts of the world.

Preparing for the storms

Meteorologists predict the speed and direction of storms and hurricanes. Then warnings are broadcast so that people in places that may be hit can protect themselves and their property.

◄ *When forecasters warned that Hurricane Ivan was heading towards Cuba, this family left their home on the coast, taking their furniture and belongings with them.*

Hurricane damage

On the Beaufort Scale of wind speeds, a hurricane is the strongest type of wind, called Force 12. It makes the sea completely white with spray and causes widespread damage on land.

Hurricanes in the news

Reports of homes and other buildings being damaged or destroyed are often front-page international news for a day or two. Remember that the effects of the hurricane last much longer than that. People's efforts to repair the damage are probably reported only in their local news.

For many reasons, news reports may not give a whole account of events. For example, some reporters were not allowed to photograph hurricane damage in one Caribbean island. Some reporters believed that the government of the island was worried that pictures of the damage would stop tourists coming to the island. The island needed the money that tourists would bring.

The Beaufort Scale

Find out about the Beaufort Scale and make a pictorial chart, showing the effects of the 12 forces of wind, on land and at sea. A useful website is www.bbc.co.uk/weather/features/az/alphabet5.shtml

Before it was hit by Hurricane Ivan, this was a five-storey building.

Weather forecasts

You can find weather reports in newspapers, on radio and TV and on news websites. They tell you what the weather has been like around the world and in your local area, and what the forecast is.

You could pick a place to compare with where you live and make a chart recording its weather and yours over a week or more.

Be a forecaster

You can begin to forecast the weather yourself, from maps like these, which tell you about the air pressure. The lines on the maps join up places where the air pressure is the same. High pressure means the weather will be fine. Low pressure means wet weather.

▲ *Weather forecasters use symbols like these to make their maps easy for people to understand.*

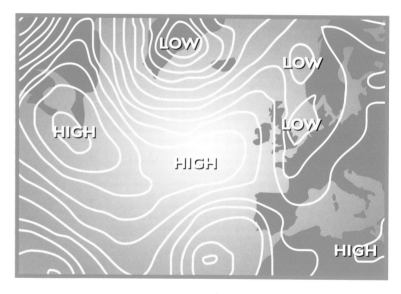

▲ *What do these two maps tell you about the*
◄ *weather where you live?*

In the Northern Hemisphere, winds blow clockwise around a high pressure area and anti-clockwise around a low pressure area. The winds are strongest where the pressure lines are closest together.

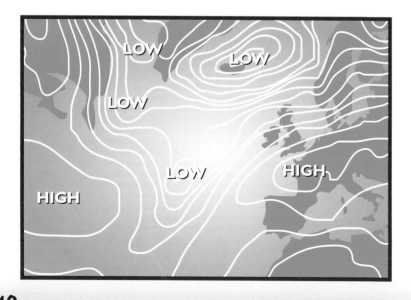

Shipping forecasts

Four times a day, British radio broadcasts a weather forecast designed especially for ships. Warnings are given of any gales. Then information is given about the wind speeds and directions, the weather, and the visibility in different areas.

▶ *Study this map as you listen to a shipping forecast. Which of the areas are forecast to have the strongest winds?*

Why are forecasts useful?

Can you think of times when you made or changed your plans because of the weather forecast? List some people who would be interested in the weather forecast because of their work. Why might you include builders, teachers and photographers?

The map shows these areas: SE Iceland, Faeroes, Bailey, Fair Isle, Viking, N. Utsire, S. Utsire, Hebrides, Cromarty, Fisher, Rockall, Malin, Forth, Forties, Dogger, Tyne, German Bight, Irish Sea, Humber, Shannon, Thames, Fastnet, Lundy, Dover, Sole, Plymouth, Wight, Portland, FitzRoy, Biscay, Trafalgar.

Time limit

Radio weather forecasters must give their reports in a limited time, such as two minutes. Can you write an interesting description of yesterday's weather which takes you exactly one minute to speak?

◀ *In wet weather, taxi drivers expect more customers. They also know that traffic is likely to be busier and slower than in dry weather.*

Global warming

Global warming is a weather issue that is often in the news. Scientists say that this rise in temperature of the earth's atmosphere could have serious effects.

What causes it?

The earth's atmosphere is made up of gases. Some of them have a similar effect to the glass of a greenhouse. They keep in some of the heat that comes from the sun, so that the earth stays warm enough for life to survive.

The problem is that, since the world became industrialised, extra greenhouse gases have

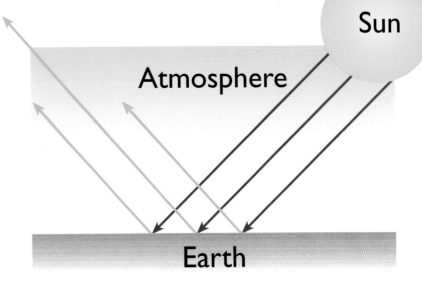

▲ *The sun's rays heat the earth and some of the heat is reflected. Greenhouse gases in the atmosphere prevent some of the reflected heat from escaping into space.*

been pumped into the atmosphere. This happens particularly when fossil fuels such as petrol and coal are burnt. Now greenhouse gases trap in more heat than before and the earth's atmosphere is a few degrees warmer.

The possible effects

Global warming could result in:

- more droughts;
- stronger hurricanes, because they are affected by the temperature of the seas;
- a rise in sea levels, because the icecaps will melt and the sea water will keep expanding as it warms up. This could lead to flooding of coastal places.

▼ *In a drought, the land becomes so dry that crops cannot grow.*

This is the island of Tuvalu in the Pacific Ocean. It has about 10,000 inhabitants. Rising sea levels could cause the island to disappear completely.

Fossil fuels

Look at www.epa.gov/globalwarming/kids/change.html. Find the names of two fossil fuels.

Can you think of two ways in which we could cut down our use of fossil fuels in our homes, to help reduce greenhouse gas emissions?

The Kyoto Protocol

At a meeting in Kyoto, Japan, in 1997, government leaders from around the world made an agreement to cut down greenhouse gas emission. The agreement is called the Kyoto Protocol. Many countries have set a target amount by which their industries will reduce the greenhouse gases they produce.

The new machinery, methods and materials needed in order to reduce greenhouse gases are expensive. This is one reason why some countries do not feel able to sign up to the Kyoto agreement.

Planting trees is good for the environment. Trees take in carbon dioxide, which is a greenhouse gas. They give out oxygen.

Volcanoes and earthquakes

Volcanic eruptions and earthquakes receive great attention in the media. At first the news may show pictures of the large numbers of people affected. Later there may be personal stories of survivors.

What are volcanoes?

Volcanoes are openings in the earth's crust through which molten rock, rock fragments, ashes, dust and gases are ejected. Volcanoes can be dormant, active or extinct. They take their name from the Roman god of fire, Vulcan.

Try to find these volcanoes on a world map:

- Mount Saint Helens, Washington, USA
- Mount Vesuvius, Italy
- Mount Fuji, Japan
- Krakatau, Indonesia
- Popocatepetl, Mexico

'I was there'

Find out about the eruption of Vesuvius, which destroyed the town of Pompeii in AD 79. Write a news article in which an imaginary survivor tells his or her story.

◄ This photograph was taken when Mount Saint Helens erupted in May 1980. You can find out about the story of this eruption by visiting http://news.bbc.co.uk and searching for Mount Saint Helens.

What are earthquakes?

Earthquakes are a shaking of the earth's surface. In a news report you might hear that an earthquake measured 6 on the Richter Scale. This is strong. An earthquake measuring 2 on the scale would not be felt.

▲ *An earthquake caused this crack in a road in California, USA.*

▶ *This map shows what scientists believe are the boundaries between the main plates of the earth's crust. Do the volcanoes and earthquakes mentioned on these pages occur near the boundaries?*

Public information

Newspapers and news broadcasts can help to inform the public about what to do in an emergency. This simple-to-remember advice is given about what to do in an earthquake:

- DROP (to the floor),
- COVER (get underneath something for protection) and
- HOLD ON.

Where do volcanoes and earthquakes happen?

The earth's crust is broken into huge fragments, called plates. They rest on the mantle and are slowly moving all the time. If the edges of the plates grind against each other, this produces earthquakes. Volcanoes can happen where the plates move apart or where they crash.

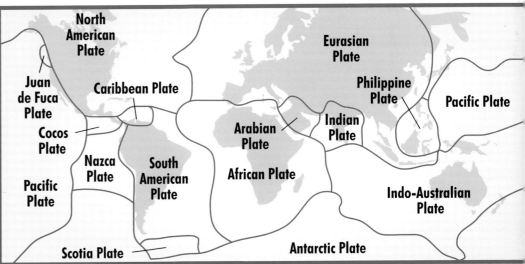

Prize-winning places

Sometimes, in local, national and international news, you may see or hear about buildings, places or displays that have won prizes.

Local prizes

Look out for local news of a 'best-kept village', an 'in-bloom competition', or a new building that has won an award for having good accessibility and being comfortable for all people to use.

▲ What do you think people should do, to help their village be judged the best-kept?

▲ 'In-bloom' competitions encourage people to use gardening to improve their local environment. Find out if your town takes part in one.

◀ This garden centre won an 'access award', because it is designed to be welcoming for customers with disabilities. Helpful features include automatic doors, a low-level counter for wheelchair users, and good lighting plus large-print signs for visually impaired people.

Judging buildings

For many competitions there is a group of judges who must agree on their decisions. Judges of buildings will consider:

- how well the buildings fit in with those already there. This includes looking at each building's size, shape and style, and the materials it is made from.

- whether the buildings are environmentally friendly. For example, have they been designed so that the amount of energy needed for lighting and heating is kept to a low level?

- accessibility or how easy or difficult it is for all members of the public to use the buildings.

Award some medals

Look at your local area and list three buildings which you think could be awarded gold, silver and bronze medals. Try to photograph them and display the photographs, with the medals, on your classroom news board.

The Stirling Prize

Each autumn you may see news of the Stirling Prize. This is awarded to the British architect of the building that the judges think is the best new building of the year.

In 2004 the winner of the Stirling Prize was Norman Foster, the architect of this building in London. Its shape has led people to call it 'the gherkin'.

17

Changes to the local area

Look for news articles about building plans in your locality and find the places on a local map. Plans are announced in the 'Public Notices' section of local newspapers, and the 'Letters' page often includes people's opinions about proposed changes. Listen for opinions on local radio and TV too.

Planning permission

People may want to build new houses, community buildings, offices, factories or power stations. They may want to change their shop front, turn land into a sports ground, widen a road, put up a mobile telephone mast or set up a wind farm. But before any building work begins, plans must be drawn up and submitted to the local planning authority.

▶ *Many people feel that mobile phone masts spoil the appearance of an area. They also worry about possible health dangers from the radio waves that the mast transmits.*

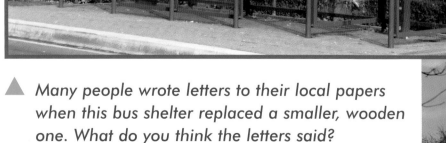

▲ *Many people wrote letters to their local papers when this bus shelter replaced a smaller, wooden one. What do you think the letters said?*

▼ *Wind power is a clean and renewable energy source for making electricity. But some people dislike the appearance and noise of wind farms.*

The planning authority writes to people who live close to where the new building would be, to ask for their comments. Announcements and articles in the media keep the general public informed. It is important to give everyone the opportunity to express their opinions about changes that would affect their lives.

The planning authority takes all opinions into account before deciding whether or not to permit a building project to go ahead. Often the plans must be changed and resubmitted.

Objections

People feel strongly about changes to their environment. They may be worried about:

- buildings being ugly;
- greenbelt land being used for building;
- the destruction of buildings they valued;
- noise;
- inconvenience.

What other objections do people make? What could be done to lessen their worries?

Differing views

Find out about a building project that is causing controversy in your local area. Write what you think two people with different views would say if they were interviewed on a local news programme. Role-play the interviews.

Protecting wildlife

You may have heard the expression, 'It's all doom and gloom.' Often news stories are gloomy. Why do you think this is?

However, good news is reported, such as babies being born, people rescued from danger, money raised for charity and people giving their time to help others. Here are examples of good news stories about animals.

RETURN OF THE OTTERS

Otters had died out in many English rivers, but now their numbers are increasing. It is largely thanks to the water companies' work to clean up our rivers.

BADGERS REHOUSED

Builders were concerned that badger setts would need to be destroyed to clear the site for a new road. So they made new setts in a safer place and laid bait to attract the badgers. They did not start work on the road until the badgers were settled in their new homes.

Endangered species

Look for 'good news' stories about saving endangered animals. Try searching www.worldwildlife.org/endangered. Design a poster about one of the animals to explain the importance of this work.

A HOPEFUL SIGN

Pandas are in danger of extinction, because so much of China's bamboo forest where they live has been cut down. But a survey has counted 1,500 pandas in China. That is 500 more than expected.

▶ *The only places where pandas live are the bamboo forests of China. Pandas depend entirely on bamboo for their food and so, if the bamboo forest is destroyed, the pandas starve.*

Why should we protect plants and animals?

Many human activities change the natural environment, in ways that damage the habitats of animals and plants. If too much of a habitat is destroyed, wildlife species that lived there may become extinct. It is important to value and protect plants and animals from extinction for the following reasons.

- They add interest, colour and beauty to our planet.

- They may provide useful medicines.

- Animals play an important part in plant reproduction when they eat the plants and deposit the seeds in a new place, in their dung.

- Plants and animals are important to each other as they all form part of food chains.

Countryside concerns

People who live in the country sometimes like to visit a town for shopping or entertainment. People from towns visit the country for walks and to enjoy the scenery and peace. Sadly we sometimes see news reports of disputes between the two groups. The problems usually arise because country and town people do not always understand each other's way of life or the difficulties each experiences.

House prices

You may find news about houses in country places. Some richer townspeople like to buy a holiday home in the country. They can afford to pay high prices, and so the price of houses in the country goes up. Some local people then cannot afford a house in their own area.

Village communities

You may find news about a small village school that is going to close. Children in the village will have to travel to a larger school, further away. You may read about village shops, banks and post offices being shut down because they do not have many customers.

Try making a list of the effects this will have on the village people's daily life.

The people of Tilford village keep their shop and post office open by working there as volunteers.

This poster outside Tilford village shop says 'Your village needs you'. It is based on a poster from the First World War, which said 'Your country needs you' and asked for men to join the army.

Farmers

Sometimes there is news about farmers and other country people taking part in demonstrations. Many farmers feel that the government in London does not understand the difficulties they have, to make a living.

Recently the subject of fox-hunting has been in the news. In 2004 Parliament voted for a law to ban fox-hunting. Many farmers and other country people are against this law. They argue that hunting helps to control the number of foxes, which kill farm animals. They also say that the ban takes jobs away from the country people who look after the hunt dogs and horses.

Ramblers

The law in the UK allows people to walk across large parts of the countryside. Sometimes there are disputes between ramblers and farmers or country landowners. Farmers worry that their animals and crops may be harmed by the visitors.

▲ These farmers marched to the Houses of Parliament in London, to draw attention to the problems they want the government to solve.

The Country Code

A set of rules called the Country Code helps us to understand how to protect the countryside and stay safe there. The key words in the code are RESPECT-PROTECT-ENJOY. Find out more by visiting www.countrysideaccess.gov.uk.

Rich and poor

There is a huge contrast between the world's richest and poorest countries. See if you can find pictures in the news that show this contrast.

The USA, the UK and other countries in Western Europe are rich countries. One main reason why they are rich is that industries developed there and became successful, selling goods around the world.

▲ This mother is comforting her son, who is weak from starvation. They live in Somalia, in Africa.

◀ This photograph appeared in a news report in the USA, saying that businesses were making profits as people bought presents for Christmas.

Why are countries poor?

The poorest countries are mostly in the Tropics. This is the area of the earth on either side of the equator, between two imaginary lines called the Tropic of Cancer and the Tropic of Capricorn. There are many reasons for the countries' poverty including:

- Weather. Crops are damaged by floods, droughts, hurricanes and other severe tropical weather. It can take years for communities to recover from these disasters.

- Wars. Governments spend huge amounts of money on weapons and armies, instead of spending on health care or education.

- Unfair trading. The richer countries buy foods like coffee, chocolate and bananas from the tropical countries, but for many years they have not paid the farmers a fair price.

What can we do?

There are no easy solutions but many people work hard to try to help. You may have taken part in Blue Peter projects or events like Red Nose Day and Children In Need, which raise money to help poor countries. Perhaps you have had a sale or done a sponsored swim, spell or walk.

Perhaps your family buys food that is labelled 'Fair trade'. This means that the farmers who produced the food have been paid a fair price.

▲ *Many supermarkets now sell 'Fair trade' foods. They include coffee, tea, chocolate, cocoa, bananas, sugar and orange juice.*

Comparing prices

Next time you go to the supermarket with mum or dad, take a notebook and pencil with you. Look for 'Fair trade' foods like coffee, sugar or bananas and write down their prices. Then find the price of the same products without the 'Fair trade' mark. Check that the quantities are the same in each case. Which costs more? Can you think why?

Do you believe it?

April 1st is April Fools' Day and many newspapers and news programmes join in the tradition of trying to trick people for fun. On that day they print or broadcast a made-up story and see how people react to it.

Spaghetti harvest

A famous April Fools' story was broadcast on the BBC *Panorama* programme in 1957. It said that Switzerland was enjoying an excellent spaghetti harvest, thanks to mild weather. Pictures showed people pulling strings of spaghetti down from trees. Many people believed the story and some telephoned the BBC to ask how they could grow spaghetti too.

◀ *Spaghetti is a type of pasta, which is made from flour dough.*

Motorway rules

In 1991, some people believed a report about new rules to reduce traffic jams on the M25. Find this circular motorway on a road map. The report said that on some weekdays all the traffic must drive clockwise around the motorway. On other days all the traffic must drive anti-clockwise.

Some of the people who believed this report complained strongly. Can you work out why they were cross? Look at the road map and imagine travelling from Rickmansworth to King's Langley on an anti-clockwise day.

◀ *What real solutions do you know about for reducing traffic jams on motorways?*

A heat-giving plant

On 1 April 1995, it was reported that Professor Olaf Lipro had discovered a plant that gave out heat and could be used for central heating. Try rearranging the letters of his name!

Be alert!

Even when it is not April 1st, you should be careful about believing news stories. Reporters try to give a true account of events, but no single report can tell you the whole story. Remember:

- There may not be room or time for all details to be given.

- Stories and pictures are chosen for their dramatic impact.

- A report may not give you all points of view. Newspapers and news programmes are often biased to one point of view.

Mine included some stories about the people who were evacuated before the hurricane.

The one I read talked about how fast the hurricane was travelling.

Compare papers

Agree with some friends that on a given day you will each bring a national paper from the previous day. Choose an important story from that day and compare how it was reported in the different papers. Was it on the front page in every paper? Were the facts the same in each?

Glossary

accessibility   how easy a place is to approach, enter or use.

active   of a volcano: likely to erupt.

air pressure   how much the particles of gases which make up the air press against everything around them. Air pressure is measured with a barometer.

architect   someone qualified to design buildings and supervise their construction.

Beaufort Scale   a scale describing the effects of different wind speeds, invented in 1806 by Admiral Francis Beaufort.

biased   leaning to one side of a debate, rather than having a balanced view.

broadcast   to pass on information or entertainment, on TV or radio.

community   the people living in a particular area.

county   one of the many parts into which the UK is divided, for example: Cornwall, Cumbria, Dyfed, Norfolk, Berkshire.

crops   plants grown for a particular purpose, especially to provide food.

crust   the outer shell of the earth.

deforestation   the cutting down and burning of large areas of trees, in places such as the Amazonian rainforests.

demonstrations   meetings, marches and other actions by groups of people who join together to show that they are protesting about something.

dormant   sleeping; a dormant volcano is one that is not active at the moment, but it is not extinct.

drought   a long period without rainfall.

emission   the release of something (e.g. gases) into the environment.

endangered   in danger of becoming extinct.

environment   the surroundings in which people, plants and animals live.

environmentally friendly   designed to be good for the environment or not to damage it.

equator   an imaginary line around the centre of the earth. Every point on this line is equally distant from the north and south poles.

evacuated   removed from a dangerous place.

extinct   died out. An extinct volcano is no longer capable of erupting.

food chain   a set of plants and living creatures which are linked because each one is food for the next in the chain.

forecast   a prediction of what will happen.

fossil fuels   coal, oil and natural gas, which were formed in the earth hundreds of millions of years ago, before the time of the dinosaurs.

CAIRN ENERGY
BEST KEPT
VILLAGE
WINNERS CLASS
CHURT
1996

gales   winds of force 8 on the Beaufort Scale. Force 9 is a strong gale.

greenbelt   open land surrounding a town.

habitat	the normal place where a plant or animal finds what it needs to survive.
hurricanes	Force 12 winds on the Beaufort Scale.
hypothermia	when a person's body temperature drops very low, and the body's organs no longer work properly.
icecaps	permanent sheets of ice covered with snow, in the polar regions.
industrialised	involved in large-scale manufacturing, mining or extraction of raw materials and the construction of factories in which to carry out this work.
local planning authority	the group in your local council which looks at proposals for new buildings. They either give or refuse permission for building to begin.
locality	the area around a particular place.
mantle	the part of the earth between the crust and the core.
media	newspapers, radio and television.
meteorologists	scientists who study the earth's atmosphere in order to be able to forecast the weather.
molten	liquefied or melted.
Northern hemisphere	the northern part of the earth, above the equator.
poles	the north pole and the south pole are the two ends of the axis around which the earth rotates. The north pole always points to the star, Polaris.
pollution	the poisoning of rivers, lakes, seas and the atmosphere, for example by fumes from burning fossil fuels and by waste products from industry.
ramblers	people who go walking for pleasure.
reproduction	the way that new plants or living creatures come into being, the same as the ones before.
Richter Scale	a scale for measuring the strength of earthquakes.
sett	a badger's burrow.
species	a group of living things with the same characteristics.
submitted	handed in (e.g. a plan or report), so that it can be considered (e.g. by a local planning authority).
tornadoes	nature's fiercest storms with wind speeds of up to 250 mph.
Tropical	from the Tropics, an area of the earth between a line called the Tropic of Cancer, north of the equator, and a line called the Tropic of Capricorn, south of the equator.
visibility	the distance around that someone can see. E.g. in fog, visibility is poor.
volunteer	someone who does a job for no payment.
wind farm	a large group of wind-driven generators for electricity supply.

For teachers and parents

This book is designed to help children at the upper end of KS2 to achieve the learning outcomes set out in Unit 16 of the QCA Geography Scheme of Work.

News items from all sources can be an excellent stimulus for Geography work, especially on specific topics within the two general themes of the Weather and Environmental Change. The examples in this book show how typical news stories through the year can lead into work that helps to develop children's skills in:

- locating places on maps;
- using maps, atlases and globes;
- using secondary sources for background research;
- using ICT to access information;
- communicating, presenting and analysing weather data;
- understanding the impact of weather on human activity;
- understanding similarities and differences between places;
- appreciating the quality of an environment;
- communicating and explaining issues.

Many cross-curricular links can also be made, for example with literacy (including speaking and listening), ICT (including photography), citizenship and PSHE.

SUGGESTED FURTHER ACTIVITIES

Pages 4-5 Geography in the news
Ask the children to bring in the front pages of any local papers which come into their homes and perhaps front pages of papers from other areas, obtained from relatives or friends. Discuss the names of papers and their meaning: e.g. Advertiser, Voice, Observer, Argus.

To help increase the children's awareness of where places are, ask them to bring in news cuttings of stories from around the world and pin these up around a large world map. Link each story with coloured thread to the corresponding place on the map.

Encourage the children to find information in local papers about recent and proposed changes to buildings or to roads/traffic. Find the places mentioned on local street maps.

Pages 6-7 The weather in the news
Visit www.bbc.co.uk/paintingtheweather with the children and look at paintings of weather in all its moods. Discuss how the artist has captured the atmosphere by the use of colour, shape and texture. Talk

about some weather stories which have made the headlines recently or within the children's memory. Ask the children to paint their own picture of one of these.

The news item about floods in Boscastle could stimulate work on the causes of flooding. Search www.google.com for 'global warming' or 'floods'.

Another issue in the news has been the paving over of gardens to make them low maintenance or to create hard standing for cars, and the effect of this on land drainage. The children could try to design a low-maintenance garden which combines hard standing and planted areas.

Pages 8-9 The hurricane season
www.fema.gov/kids/hurr.htm is a good child-friendly site including information and interactive games related to hurricanes.

Pages 10-11 Weather forecasts
Some interesting maths work could be included here. Children could collect data about the weather in their area over a given period and use the data to make graphs. They might also enjoy comparing weather forecasts with what actually happens.

www.bbc.co.uk/weather/weatherwise/activities has excellent ideas for things to make, including a weather vane and barometer, as well as information on how to create static electricity.

Perhaps you could make a class display about people whose work is influenced by the weather.

Record the late night shipping forecast (Radio 4, 00:48) over 2/3 days and use it with the children, asking them to imagine that they are listening to it on a ship. Talk about the importance of the set format in which this forecast is given. Maps of shipping forecast areas are on www.gwp.enta.net/mailfax00.htm or www.gwp.enta.net/shipmap.htm.

Pages 12-13 Global warming
Explore the history of deforestation in the British Isles. The process began with the arrival of the first farmers some time before 4000 BC.

Use www.ukagriculture.com/countryside/history_of_countryside/countryside_history.html. Ask the children to click on each century in chronological order, and list the descriptions they find under 'Climate'.

Ask the children to find out about three inventions from the Industrial Revolution (e.g. Thomas Newcomen's steam engine, James Hargreaves' 'spinning Jenny' or George Stephenson's steam locomotive) and discuss the implications of increased industry on the environment.

Pages 14-15 Volcanoes and earthquakes
After finding the volcanoes on a world map it might be helpful for the children to repeat the exercise using a globe.

The story of the eruption of Vesuvius in AD 79 and the destruction of Pompeii could be useful material for a literacy session prior to the children attempting the writing activity.

Pages 16-17 Prize-winning places
Children might try designing a feature for their town or a building which they think would win a prize for its function or its appearance.

Discuss how litter and graffiti might affect a town's chances of winning a prize. Take the children to the high street and make a survey of litter and graffiti. Perhaps each group could count pieces of litter in a given length of pavement, or graffiti on a given length of wall. Afterwards help the children to devise a way of recording their results on a local street map.

Information about the Stirling Prize can be found at www.architecture.com.

Pages 18-19 Changes in the local area
Investigate the current distribution of wind farms in the UK. See www.bwea.com/map or www.yes2wind.com. The children should notice a greater density of farms in some areas. Discuss the possible reasons for this.

See if you can invite someone from the Local Planning Authority to give a short talk to the class about the processes involved in obtaining permission for new buildings or other changes.

For more ideas on work about changes to the local environment, see two other books in this series: LOCAL TRAFFIC and SHOULD THE HIGH STREET BE CLOSED TO TRAFFIC?

Pages 20-21 Protecting wildlife
Beijing in China will be in the news in 2008 as host to the Olympic games. Ask the children to find China on a map, atlas or globe. Using an airline route map, ask them to name the countries and/or mountain ranges that a plane would fly over between London and Beijing.

After discussion of how habitats are destroyed to meet human needs, you might plan an assembly for the school. Issues might be:

(a) clearing of forests/hedgerows, (b) farming methods including use of pesticides (there are new rules regarding their use), (c) industrial and traffic pollution. The children might make large speech bubbles to hold up as they speak.

Pages 22-23 Countryside concerns
www.countrysideaccess.gov.uk has lots of ideas for enjoying the countryside plus the updated Countryside Code. Children might like to do their own version with illustrations.

Perhaps this page could lead to work on London and where the children's locality is, in relation to London. You might discuss people's perception of the North/South divide.

Pages 24-25 Rich and poor
Some work could be done on the idea of the global village. Children might find out about going to school in other parts of the world; or what other children do to have fun.

www.peacecorps.gov/kids has many links to help raise children's awareness of other cultures.

There are also some good opportunities for map work. E.g. Use the site to find ways of greeting people in the global village. Match the greetings to places on a large wall map and display the greetings linked with coloured thread to their place of origin.

Pages 26-27 Do you believe it?
Children might ask their parents or grandparents what was the best practical joke they can remember.

There are opportunities here for some health and safety input. E.g. pulling a chair away when someone is about to sit down could cause serious injury, as could trip wires and buckets over doors. The cleverest practical jokes are those where everyone laughs, especially the person upon whom the joke is played.

The M25 story could be used as a different way in to the teaching activity suggested in the Scheme of Work as a follow-up to listening to local traffic news, where children use maps to plan alternative routes between places.

If you are using this unit of work at the time of local or general elections, children could be encouraged to bring in leaflets from different parties. Comparisons could be made between different proposals for handling issues such as law and order, funding for education, environmental issues. Discuss any obvious examples of bias.

Index